I0102656

The DEFINITIVE Guide to Fact-based Justification for
Trump's Impeachment

The DEFINITIVE Guide to Fact-based Justification for
Trump's Impeachment

The DEFINITIVE Guide to Fact-based Justification for Trump's Impeachment

2020 Election Special Edition

By Kamala Warren

Copyright 2019 Kamala Warren. All rights reserved.

ISBN 978-1-7334381-4-8

Cover image from DepositPhotos.com #224471780

Disclaimer: After carrying out untold hours of exhaustive investigation with the intent of providing a definitive guide on the subject, it is to the best of the author's knowledge that all of the information presented in this is book is both accurate and properly attributed – hence, all of the pages are blank.

Saint Grobian Press

Salinas – Tupelo – Upland – Palmetto – Idabel – Dalhart

Check out our other great products at:

www.UnionOfTruth.org

Other books by Kamala Warren:

1- The DEFINITIVE Guide to Facts and Logic that Justify Sanctuary Cities

2- The DEFINITIVE Guide to Facts and Logic that Justify Disarming Law-Abiding Citizens

3- The DEFINITIVE Guide to Facts and Logic that Justify Mandatory Usage of Preferred Pronouns

4- The DEFINITIVE Guide to Facts and Logic that Justify Universal Basic Income

5- The DEFINITIVE Guide to Trump's Hate-Filled, Racist Remarks

6- The DEFINITIVE Guide to Trump's Treasonous Collusion and Obstruction

7- The DEFINITIVE Guide to Facts and Logic that Justify Government-Run Healthcare

8- The DEFINITIVE Guide to Fact-based Justification for Homosexual Indoctrination of Kindergarten Students

9- The DEFINITIVE Guide to Democratic Party Accomplishments in the Trump Era

10- The DEFINITIVE Guide to Cogent Liberal Talking Points

11- The DEFINITIVE Guide to Fact-based Justification for Spying on Candidate Trump

The DEFINITIVE Guide to Fact-based Justification for
Trump's Impeachment

The DEFINITIVE Guide to Fact-based Justification for
Trump's Impeachment

The DEFINITIVE Guide to Fact-based Justification for
Trump's Impeachment

The DEFINITIVE Guide to Fact-based Justification for
Trump's Impeachment

The DEFINITIVE Guide to Fact-based Justification for
Trump's Impeachment

The DEFINITIVE Guide to Fact-based Justification for
Trump's Impeachment

The DEFINITIVE Guide to Fact-based Justification for
Trump's Impeachment

The DEFINITIVE Guide to Fact-based Justification for
Trump's Impeachment

The DEFINITIVE Guide to Fact-based Justification for
Trump's Impeachment

The DEFINITIVE Guide to Fact-based Justification for
Trump's Impeachment

The DEFINITIVE Guide to Fact-based Justification for
Trump's Impeachment

The DEFINITIVE Guide to Fact-based Justification for
Trump's Impeachment

The DEFINITIVE Guide to Fact-based Justification for
Trump's Impeachment

The DEFINITIVE Guide to Fact-based Justification for
Trump's Impeachment

The DEFINITIVE Guide to Fact-based Justification for
Trump's Impeachment

The DEFINITIVE Guide to Fact-based Justification for
Trump's Impeachment

The DEFINITIVE Guide to Fact-based Justification for
Trump's Impeachment

The DEFINITIVE Guide to Fact-based Justification for
Trump's Impeachment

The DEFINITIVE Guide to Fact-based Justification for
Trump's Impeachment

The DEFINITIVE Guide to Fact-based Justification for
Trump's Impeachment

The DEFINITIVE Guide to Fact-based Justification for
Trump's Impeachment

The DEFINITIVE Guide to Fact-based Justification for
Trump's Impeachment

The DEFINITIVE Guide to Fact-based Justification for
Trump's Impeachment

The DEFINITIVE Guide to Fact-based Justification for
Trump's Impeachment

The DEFINITIVE Guide to Fact-based Justification for
Trump's Impeachment

The DEFINITIVE Guide to Fact-based Justification for
Trump's Impeachment

The DEFINITIVE Guide to Fact-based Justification for
Trump's Impeachment

The DEFINITIVE Guide to Fact-based Justification for
Trump's Impeachment

The DEFINITIVE Guide to Fact-based Justification for
Trump's Impeachment

The DEFINITIVE Guide to Fact-based Justification for
Trump's Impeachment

The DEFINITIVE Guide to Fact-based Justification for
Trump's Impeachment

The DEFINITIVE Guide to Fact-based Justification for
Trump's Impeachment

The DEFINITIVE Guide to Fact-based Justification for
Trump's Impeachment

The DEFINITIVE Guide to Fact-based Justification for
Trump's Impeachment

The DEFINITIVE Guide to Fact-based Justification for
Trump's Impeachment

The DEFINITIVE Guide to Fact-based Justification for
Trump's Impeachment

The DEFINITIVE Guide to Fact-based Justification for
Trump's Impeachment

The DEFINITIVE Guide to Fact-based Justification for
Trump's Impeachment

The DEFINITIVE Guide to Fact-based Justification for
Trump's Impeachment

The DEFINITIVE Guide to Fact-based Justification for
Trump's Impeachment

The DEFINITIVE Guide to Fact-based Justification for
Trump's Impeachment

The DEFINITIVE Guide to Fact-based Justification for
Trump's Impeachment

The DEFINITIVE Guide to Fact-based Justification for
Trump's Impeachment

The DEFINITIVE Guide to Fact-based Justification for
Trump's Impeachment

The DEFINITIVE Guide to Fact-based Justification for
Trump's Impeachment

The DEFINITIVE Guide to Fact-based Justification for
Trump's Impeachment

The DEFINITIVE Guide to Fact-based Justification for
Trump's Impeachment

The DEFINITIVE Guide to Fact-based Justification for
Trump's Impeachment

The DEFINITIVE Guide to Fact-based Justification for
Trump's Impeachment

The DEFINITIVE Guide to Fact-based Justification for
Trump's Impeachment

The DEFINITIVE Guide to Fact-based Justification for
Trump's Impeachment

The DEFINITIVE Guide to Fact-based Justification for
Trump's Impeachment

The DEFINITIVE Guide to Fact-based Justification for
Trump's Impeachment

The DEFINITIVE Guide to Fact-based Justification for
Trump's Impeachment

The DEFINITIVE Guide to Fact-based Justification for
Trump's Impeachment

The DEFINITIVE Guide to Fact-based Justification for
Trump's Impeachment

The DEFINITIVE Guide to Fact-based Justification for
Trump's Impeachment

The DEFINITIVE Guide to Fact-based Justification for
Trump's Impeachment

The DEFINITIVE Guide to Fact-based Justification for
Trump's Impeachment

The DEFINITIVE Guide to Fact-based Justification for
Trump's Impeachment

The DEFINITIVE Guide to Fact-based Justification for
Trump's Impeachment

The DEFINITIVE Guide to Fact-based Justification for
Trump's Impeachment

The DEFINITIVE Guide to Fact-based Justification for
Trump's Impeachment

The DEFINITIVE Guide to Fact-based Justification for
Trump's Impeachment

The DEFINITIVE Guide to Fact-based Justification for
Trump's Impeachment

The DEFINITIVE Guide to Fact-based Justification for
Trump's Impeachment

The DEFINITIVE Guide to Fact-based Justification for
Trump's Impeachment

The DEFINITIVE Guide to Fact-based Justification for
Trump's Impeachment

The DEFINITIVE Guide to Fact-based Justification for
Trump's Impeachment

The DEFINITIVE Guide to Fact-based Justification for
Trump's Impeachment

The DEFINITIVE Guide to Fact-based Justification for
Trump's Impeachment

The DEFINITIVE Guide to Fact-based Justification for
Trump's Impeachment

The DEFINITIVE Guide to Fact-based Justification for
Trump's Impeachment

The DEFINITIVE Guide to Fact-based Justification for
Trump's Impeachment

The DEFINITIVE Guide to Fact-based Justification for
Trump's Impeachment

The DEFINITIVE Guide to Fact-based Justification for
Trump's Impeachment

The DEFINITIVE Guide to Fact-based Justification for
Trump's Impeachment

The DEFINITIVE Guide to Fact-based Justification for
Trump's Impeachment

The DEFINITIVE Guide to Fact-based Justification for
Trump's Impeachment

The DEFINITIVE Guide to Fact-based Justification for
Trump's Impeachment

The DEFINITIVE Guide to Fact-based Justification for
Trump's Impeachment

The DEFINITIVE Guide to Fact-based Justification for
Trump's Impeachment

The DEFINITIVE Guide to Fact-based Justification for
Trump's Impeachment

The DEFINITIVE Guide to Fact-based Justification for
Trump's Impeachment

The DEFINITIVE Guide to Fact-based Justification for
Trump's Impeachment

The DEFINITIVE Guide to Fact-based Justification for
Trump's Impeachment

The DEFINITIVE Guide to Fact-based Justification for
Trump's Impeachment

The DEFINITIVE Guide to Fact-based Justification for
Trump's Impeachment

The DEFINITIVE Guide to Fact-based Justification for
Trump's Impeachment

The DEFINITIVE Guide to Fact-based Justification for
Trump's Impeachment

The DEFINITIVE Guide to Fact-based Justification for
Trump's Impeachment

The DEFINITIVE Guide to Fact-based Justification for
Trump's Impeachment

The DEFINITIVE Guide to Fact-based Justification for
Trump's Impeachment

The DEFINITIVE Guide to Fact-based Justification for
Trump's Impeachment

www.ingramcontent.com/pod-product-compliance
Lightning Source LLC
Chambersburg PA
CBHW060512280326
41933CB00014B/2941